common threads

A COLLECTION OF POETRY

Meagan -
May you find a common thread
and know that you are not alone.
CaBabl

CARA BABEL

Vikki M. Hankins™ Publishing

VMH

Vikki M. Hankins™ Publishing
3355 Lenox Rd. NE Suite 750
Atlanta, GA 30326
www.vmhpublishing.com

Manufactured in the United States of America

ISBN: 978-0-9984553-6-5

10 9 8 7 6 5 4 3 2 1

Cover Design by Vikki M. Hankins™ Publishing

The first, and only, poem that I published was titled, "Smile to Share." It was a contest that I participated in. Basically, if you submitted your poem and paid for the book, you were published. My main goal of submitting this poem was to brag that I had a copyright under my name. It was silly really, but I did it anyway. When I showed my mom the book that I overpaid for, she was shocked that I had submitted this poem. In fact she asked why I had submitted such a silly poem. She had read much of my other writing and she felt that I could have shown more of myself in my work. However, I was young and unwilling to expose myself to actual critique or praise. I was unsure of what my writing could really mean to people. As I have gotten older, I have added to my poetry. Most things I have written recently are for a special occasion but all are from within me. I share them with you now in a hope that you may find a common thread, a thought, or just a good laugh or cry. At first, I was going to organize the poetry into sections such as "love," "heartache," and "friendship." However, after reading through some of the poems, I realized that the interpretation should be left up to the reader. Therefore, there is no organized placement of the writing.

Table of Contents

CARA BABEL

common threads

CARA BABEL

Cheerleader

When I would try, to no avail

And thought that I would surely fail

I heard your voice and felt your strength

And knew I'd come through at any length

You were my cheerleader and my
encouragement

You'll never know how much your cheers
have meant.

Floating

I felt something today

    That I thought I had lost

You made me float

    And I wondered why

        Now, after you're gone, I know

You make me feel beautiful

    Because you looked at me

    And smiled

Past

You appeared out of no where

A vision of the past
And now you invade my thoughts
You revolve in my dreams
Yet your actual presence – no more
My thinking has changed
I am confused – like never before
All because you came back

Friendship

Today, here and now
Let us make this sacred vow
That our friendship will stay strong
Though the journey will be long
And the distance between us wide
Let our connection never ever hide
Even with all the changes, sure to come
Others will be more drastic than some
Let us always remain true
So I don't lose this friendship with you

The Same

If God made us all the same

Where would we be today?
There would have been no Abraham
Who took all he had
And left for unchartered water
There would have never been Noah
Who was so unlike everyone
That he was the one to survive
There would not have been Moses
Who rose up
And led
There would be no heroes
To fight the wars
To aid the misfortunate
Or to love the children
Most importantly, there'd be no you
To love, to comfort
To listen, to be
I think God had the right idea
Giving each of us our own body and mind
Because if God had made us all the same
There would be no US

Seeing

I wish you could see
What I see
    A devoted wife
    A loving mother
    A caring review
    A tremendous teacher
    An incredible human being
        That's you, Mom

Anything

I'd do anything
To see you smile
        Anything
Because you'd do
    Anything for
        Me

Hero

A mother is a hero
    Overcoming the most obscure obstacles

Diaper changing through adolescents

Devoting tremendous amounts of time

Packing lunches and quietly listening

Fighting the fiercest battles

To teach what is right and to protect

Sacrificing her life only to see her child
smile

No hero can out-do the heroism of a mother

And yet a mother receives, nor wishes to
receive, a medal

For her courage and heroism

I Saw You

I used to dream of life and what my future
held

Of all the little things and how they would
weld

Into a life I could call my own

In a large city or a tiny town

Every vision contained a man

Whom I loved with all a woman can

I never knew who the man was

Just saw an outline in gentle fuzz

I have had my guesses to who it could be

Though his face I could never see
And finally I knew last night
When your face appeared in the glowing light

Pain

I felt a pain last night
Stronger than I've ever felt before
It was deep within my soul
I thought my heart was breaking
This morning when I woke up
I looked deep into my being
And saw my heart, unbroken
What was the pain then?
My heart was still strong
Then it hit me
I could see my unbroken heart so clearly
Because there was no wall
Like there used to be
My heart was free
You did that for me
You destroyed what I had built
To protect and hide behind
I now lay vulnerable

Just like you wanted

Now you could see my heart

For what it really was

And so, I turn to you

To show you your victory

But you are not there

And so, alone, I sit here

Putting the pieces back

Rebuilding the wall

So no one can hurt me

Like you did

The Wall

I have built a great wall

So tall, you cannot climb it

So wide, you cannot traverse around it

So thick, you cannot push it down

It guards my most prized procession

This wall I have built

It is not made of stone

    Nor brick

    Nor wood

Its foundation is strong with pride

The rest, is composed of

    Past heartaches

    Hopes, dreams, desires

    Fear – of the past and what may come

    Hardships and hate

Each element was placed with passion

A devotion so strong, to protect what lie behind

You simply wait silently until the day comes

    When I let my heart be free

Fear

I was afraid then

As I am now

But I have chosen

    To swallow my pride

Tell you how I feel

    Risk getting hurt

I love it when you kiss me

    On my lips, my neck, my back

I adore how you pull me into you

    As soon as you wake up

I love it when I catch you

Watching me from across the room
I adore your smile
Meant only for me to see
And even if you can't see it
It's everything about you
So, there it is
And here I am afraid
To be happy

Belief in Love

They've said that some things
Have to be believed to be seen
And this is the case with love
Because without a belief in love
The smiles are just involuntary
The kindness is merely a trick
The passion is only an act
And the heart is simply an organ
But once you believe, you truly believe in love
The smile becomes an expression
The kindness becomes the world
The passion becomes real

And the heart becomes full

Falling

I could never let myself fall
That would be a loss of control
And I wanted to remain in control
So I allowed myself to drift
Aimlessly, unhappily, alone
Until you made me lose control
As I finally fell in love

Love's Power

How can you love
Something so heartless
That cannot love you back
Is unwilling to love anything
You knew this and still you loved
Because you knew its power
As I refused to see

Movie

I wish life was a movie
Where we could fast forward
As well as rewind
Where we saw the whole picture
Everyone's side, exposed
Then maybe I could be happy
Because then, I would have the remote

Control

Control is a crazy thing
Just when you think you own it
It changes and you lose your grasp
Only when you allow it to be free
Can you make a rational choice

Right

You asked me what scared me
Then you list my every fear
    You were right
It is the way you hold me

Never wanting to let go
It is the way you look at me
So gentle and yearning
It is the way you kiss me
When you think that I am asleep
It is the way you smile at me
So pure and caring
You were right
I AM terrified
Because it seems so right
You were right
Because you are so right

Incredible You

I watch you and wonder
What did I do to deserve
Such happiness
What great task did I accomplish
To receive such a great reward
I stop and stare at this great gift
And wonder this for a second
But only a second do I stop
Then I wrap my arms around you

So I won't lose this
Incredible You

To Be You

You are everything I want to be
But I can't let you know it
Even if you don't see it
I listen to your every word
Watch your every action
And imitate each
Because I want to be like you

Imitation

When I fail and fall short
My glory is lost
And yours too, is gone forever
You are perfection
I am far from it
Only a cheap imitation

Faith

You put so much faith in me
You think I can do the impossible
And sometimes I can; miracles do happen
But I also fall short
Short of the victory
    And short, it seems, to your faith
I can handle letting myself down
But you – how can I?
How can anyone let down the only thing
You're fighting to uphold?

A Thank You

I cried in your arms
    And you held me
I yelled at you
    And you forgot about it
I was mean and stupid
    And you forgave me
I did nothing to deserve your love
    But still you give it
Endlessly and unconditionally

Thank you

Again

I can't even cry
I have no emotion
    I've used it all previously
So I go on, unexpressful and leading
Because I just can't go through it
    Not again

Her/Me

I can't help but wonder
If you like her more
    You laugh with her
    You sing crazy songs together
    You can talk about the same thing forever
    Worst of all, you have so much fun
And I sit watching
    I try to join in
    But I don't understand the jokes
    I don't know the words
    I'm tongue tied

So I watch
The two people I love most
Like each other more and more

Betrayal

I said it would never happen again
I wouldn't make that mistake twice
Never, I promised myself
To lie is horrific
But to betray yourself; unforgivable

Requests

I never ask for much
Maybe just a hug
You normally comply
And wrap your arms around me
- Thank you for that
Now, all I ask you for is to listen
It doesn't require any energy
Only quiet
But you can't give me that
Why? It's so much easier

Caring

You act like you don't care
    That's a good trait
      Sometimes
But when you have that attitude
Towards someone you claim to love
    Then it must not be love
Only something not to care about

Best

You think you know what's best
    In the past, you've been right
But now, trust in your teachings
    And let me choose
Because I know what I want
    And with your earlier guidance
    I know what's best

Search

It's not supposed to be a job
You shouldn't feel obligated

It should be done because
> It's what you want
>> What you've always wanted
> Sure, it might not be as
>> Perfect as your dreams

Love is what you make of it
I want to make it your dream for you
> Yet you won't tell me your dreams
>> And leave me helplessly
>>> Searching for love

Lost & Found

By leaving all who I thought were close
And venturing into uncharted territory
With the help of new friends
And without the distraction of old friends
> I found myself
>> And I didn't even know I was lost

Tiny Miracles

So many things, each day, go unnoticed
Almost as if things are taken for granted

Like a smile

Or a touch

Or a kiss

Or a look of longing

But when you meet someone the first time,

You notice everything

Their smell

Their eyes, always watching you

Their lips, soft and luring

Everything!

It is the same for someone you love

Everyday something new surfaces

A tiny miracle appears

And you fall in love with them again

The following two poems were written in memory of my Grandmother who was the organist at our church for over 60 years. She had no formal training but her music was incredible. She always played with one shoe off and it was a race between my sister and I to see who got to help her put her shoe back on at the end of the service. To my Grandma who taught me so much about selflessness.

Angel

It has been said that angels do exist

They're dressed in white, with halos above their heads

Maybe so, but a true angle wears slacks and doesn't have a halo

A real angle sits on a bench, with one shoe off, waiting for her cue

A real angle does her job without a big fancy scene

A real angel is quiet and sometimes even unnoticed

A real angel is a Grandma

Loving Fingers

Every week, she took a stroll

All alone, yet in a crowd

She was determined to make 'em stand

With a single note, all would rise

And she would play, like an angel

Love poured from her fingertips

And while the music may stop

The love never will

Piece By Piece

Like a puzzle, with one piece missing,
　　I lie here
All the corners are there
　　You see the basic shape
But it's still not complete
　　One piece is missing
You try, piece by piece
　　Nothing works
But you don't give up
　　You keep trying
　　　Piece by piece
You become frustrated
　　And you pound
　　　Piece by piece
Then you wonder, if there is a piece
　　To fill the hole
So you lay down next to me
　　And fill my heart
　　　The missing piece!

Without

You cannot appreciate love
>   Without dreading hate
You cannot experience happiness
>   Without knowing sadness
You cannot have
>   Without longing
You cannot die
>   Without living first

Already Given

There are no tears

To grant comfort

There are no arms

To hold securely

There are no words

To give encouragement

Except for those which you have already given

They will come back to you

>   To comfort, to hold, and to encourage

Just as you did

First Sight

Love at first sight is great
It's the love that is also at
    Fourth, eighteenth, and millionth time
      That survives

Not Knowing

I knew, from day one,
That this day would come
And I knew then, as I do now,
    That I can't stop you
    I don't want to
What I didn't know was
    How proud I'd be
    How scared I'd be
    And how much love I'd send with you

Catcher

The catcher doesn't get the credit he deserves
No one knows all the needs that he serves
A cheerleader, an enforcer

No one is ever hoarser
From all the yelling
And all of the telling
Of who goes where
"No, not here – there"
The pitcher can't chose
His own pitch or he'd lose
It's the catcher's job to call
A curve, a change, or a fastball
The catcher takes all the heat
When a runner slides and all he sees is feet
If the ball's in the dirt
The catcher blocks it, even if it will hurt
He's the toughest player in the game
He works the hardest and doesn't complain
I'm quite proud of that guy behind the plate
Even if others don't think he's prime rate

Won't Give Up

I wouldn't give up one day
   Not to have known you
I wouldn't give up one day
   Not to have kissed you

I wouldn't give up one day

    Not to have laughed with you

And I won't give up one day with you

    To not have to say good-bye

Good-bye and Hello

Yes, this is a good-bye

    But good-byes are like chocolate

        They never last long

Good-byes are like mints

    They, too, are short-lived

And this good-bye too

    Will be short, because I will see you every day

In my heart

    My soul

    My thoughts

    My dreams

And our hellos

Backed Away

I'm sorry that I backed away

Maybe then it won't hurt as much
I'm sorry that I pull into myself
    Maybe then I won't be as lonely
I'm sorry that I pull away from you
    Maybe then I won't miss you as much
But I will try to show my love
    Maybe then I won't have to worry.

The Show

If it were to end
Whose heart would break?
Not the eagle's – who'd be free at least
I doubt the angelic boy would shutter
But those that watch – and envy
They'd cry magnificently
Their hopes; lost
Their dreams; diminished
Their fantasy; destroyed
That's why
    The show must go on
To protect those – that aren't involved

Laughing

When you came home, crying
I never laughed at you
I never made fun
And I never made you feel foolish
So, why do you laugh at me?

How

How can you judge
After all the people you've hurt
How dare you laugh at me
When all I've done is cry for you

Rescue

I wish I could rescue you
    From all harm and hurt
I wish I could rescue you
    From this torturous world
I wish I could rescue you
    From the endless demands
I wish I could rescue you

From all the cruel words
But I can't
All I can do is promise
> Not to harm or hurt
> Not to curse you
> Not to demand
> And always to love you

Cruel Words

I would gladly let them strike me
Than to watch you
> Ripped apart
> > By their cruel words

Abused

Daily beaten – yet no bruises appear

Daily harassed – yet no physical anguish

Daily devastated – yet each day you remain strong

That is abuse – but not physical

There are no fists, no kicks

Merely words, looks, and the lack of both

Sticks & Stones

As kids we'd recite

"Sticks and stones will break my bones

But words'll never hurt me"

This is true – for maybe a single cruel word

But cruel word – day after day

    Hour after hour

Can destroy even the most

    Loving, caring, enduring, forgiving
    personality

These words can destroy an individual

      Like they have me

Curse

It's a curse

Nothing is worse

Than to be smart

With a really big heat

Always giving

Instead of living

Never getting

Always fretting

Quite few friends
Always making amends
Seeing and knowing this
Giving up personal bliss
For nothing whatsoever
Alone, now and forever

Another's

To walk in another's shoes
To have another's thoughts
To live another's life
    Just for a day
To learn about yourself

Game

I don't play the game for myself
    That would be selfish
I play because God gave me the ability
And you gave me the opportunity

Distance

Distance may separate our touch
Miles may hinder our kisses
Time zones may weaken our glances
But love overcomes all these
   Obstacles and brings a person close

Awake

Awake, awake, I say
No more shall you sleep
I'll haunt you with my misery
And frighten you with doubt
I'll tear apart your heart
Eat away your soul
Leave nothing left
 But hate and cruelty
Then you shall be beat

Mine

My thoughts
My words

Mean nothing to you
To me
    They speak novels

Speaking Souls

I wish you would just hold me – silently
Your warm, moist breath on my neck
The back of your fingers glide along my arm
Just to reassure my being
Still there is silence
Because a soul needs no words

It

It plagues me
It makes me vomit
It irks my entire being
It's endless and relentless
It's you and your inability
    To understand

Maybe

Maybe it's not meant to be
This isn't our destiny
And maybe it should end
My dear, sweet friend
Maybe then we'll see
What is truly meant to be

There's More

I never thought I'd say this
But today I give my very last kiss
And then I shall leave
Possibly then you'll believe
That I must go
If only to let you know
There's more to life and love
And so much more above

Chance

I'd say I'm sorry – but I'm not
A chance of a lifetime – can't be passed up

At least not this chance

Please, understand

And give this chance

    A chance

<u>Let Go</u>

Like a little boy – that clutches his blanket

Like a dog – that won't let go of the bone

Like a toddler – that clenches his mother's apron

Like you

    That attaches to me

    So tight

    That I can't breathe

Someday, the boy will let go of the blanket

    The dog will tire of its bone

    And the toddler will loosen his grip

You, too, must loosen yours

    Because

    I will not leave you

    I'll always be near

If not in person,

    In heart and soul

Spotlight

I was always in the spotlight

I was strong, confident, and successful

So, there I stood – in the spotlight

But it shouldn't have been me

So, take my hand and join me

Because without your strength

        I am weak

Without your praise

        I lack confidence

Without your encouragement

        I don't even try

Without you

        I am nothing

You deserve the spotlight

      The one that's always been on me

Because I am nothing

        Without you

Free

It feels so good

    To be free

I can do whatever
Whenever
And with whomever
I choose
It is my right
To be free
And you can no longer take that
From me

Without You

I was doing great without you
I've never been more happy
-       Than that time away
But now, it's different
Now I'm with you but without you
And it simply doesn't work that way
So, let's go back
To how it was
Without all the confusion
And most importantly
Without you

Who Hurts

Do what is right

But how do you know

- What is right

There seems no answer

Because there is none

Either way

Someone gets hurt

So, now the question is

Who do you hurt

- The one who has already
  hurt you

- Or you, yourself

Leave Please

Why won't you just leave

And let me be

It didn't work before

And it won't work now

Not now or ever

So please

-    Leave

Easy?

It's easy to say and tough to do

To actually and finally get rid of you

So all I do is talk and wait

Until that never coming date

When you finally decide that we're through

Choose Sides

Nowhere to go –

No place to hide

All signs point one way

But my heart won't take that path

And so I choose

-    To side with my heart

In doing so, it gets broken

I know that

And so does the heart

If it can be brave

I can too

And so I choose
-      To side with my heart
Because it is right

Forgive and Forget

Can you forgive me
    That's what you asked
It's a simple, plain question
Can you forgive me
    So simple and yet so complex
I can forgive you
    But can you forgive me
If I can't forget

True

We say one thing
    And do the other
Always and forever
    We confuse another
We should just be true
    Even if it's mean

But most of all

Be true to your own being

Satellite

Like a satellite

Knocked out of orbit

I'm getting mixed signals

And giving many more

- Mixed signals

Spinning and spinning

- Out of control

In space

The truth will put the satellite

Back in orbit

And your understanding

Will set the signals right

Trapped

Now I know how it feels

And it feels terrible

I no longer know where to go

Who to turn to

I'm trapped

With no way out

And there's no one to help me

Dead Wrong

I thought I was right

But I was wrong

Dead wrong

And now the truth

Is killing me too

Believe and It'll Be True

If you believe you were wrong

It doesn't matter how right you really were

If you believe you are ugly

A troll wouldn't be attracted

If you believe you are dumb

You cannot be taught

If you believe you aren't good enough

    Then you aren't

But

If you believe that you are right

    Then you are

If you believe that you are pretty

    No one can say less

If you believe you are smart

    You will learn so much

If you believe you're good enough

    Then you're worth more than all the gold

If you believe in yourself

    Then you truly are you

And that's a great person to be

Believe

If you just say you're okay

    You won't be

If you just act like it's okay

    It won't be

Only when you believe

    It's okay

Is it really

So believe

Perfect Day

- A smile
- A word
- A glance
- A perfect day

That's all it takes

Accept You

You do so much

- To be accepted

You try so hard

- To be accepted

But, if you can't first

Accept yourself

Then no one else will

Join

Make a statement

Smile a lot

Laugh a lot

Have fun a lot

And others, too

Will see your fun

And will join you

Happy

Be happy

Do what it takes, no matter what

-    To be happy

That's what they'd say

Be happy

And now I have the chance

-    To be happy at last

But they won't let me

Thank You Friend

You've always been there
> Even through the rotten times

You listened with utmost care
> When I did my pantomimes

And for that I thank you
> My comforting friend

You remained true
> True, forever, till the end

Someday I hope to return
> All the kindness you've shown

I hope I can learn
> Everything you've already known

Hero

You've been my hero since day one
> I wanted so much to be like you

You were always having fun
> And so now, everything you do

I watch and hope that when all is done

You will like me too

Large Rewards

A drop of water
    Can bring life back to a flower
A tiny plankton
    Is the beginning of the food chain
A little smile
    Can brighten one's day
Such tiny things
    Bring such large rewards

Mature?

You say I am immature
    Define mature – please
Because a child who sees
    A dog, walking alone
        -   Walks with it
An adult, seeing that same dog
        -   Walks away
    Who's mature

A child sees a friend's tears

-     And cries with them

An adult, confronted with tears,

-     Turns and runs

Who's mature

So, go ahead and call

Me immature, but remember

You will walk alone

And cry alone

Because you aren't mature

Enough to understand

Help

Thank you for sticking up for me

I know you don't like getting involved

But you took that risk today

And just knowing that you're there for me

-     Helps

Already Known

Some friends you can tell your dreams

Some, your inner most secret

Others, your deepest fear

But to your sister, you tell nothing

Because she already knows

Free to Live

You strive for freedom

But become bonded

Bound to yourself

In your quest

Of freedom

In order to be free

You must first strive

To live

My Fault

It's what they said to do

They said it was

-    The right thing

But once I did it

- Just like they told me

It became wrong

And they blamed me

Blurred Vision

I looked at you

- Through my tears

All was blurred

I did not see you

For yourself

Now, as I look back

With dry eyes

I see you, the real one

And now I realize

Why I was

Crying to

Begin

With

Dreams

Ever since I knew you

You've been my dream

One I never want to wake up from

And now that dream comes when

I am awake

- It's finally reality

Now, there are faults and pain

Please, just let me sleep

And have dreams

Dreams that are mine

And mine alone

Inner Child

Things used to be so simple

Hop-scotch and buggars

Were our biggest concern

Nothing phased us

We were always happy

Now, as we grow older

More worries run through our head

And more time taken to better
ourselves

We rarely ever smile

Find that inner child

And be happy again

Clay

I was clay in your hands

You molded me in your vision

And now that you are done

- You look with disgust

And you blame the clay

Yet with that same clay

Someone else sculpted pure beauty

Rain

Rain is replenishing

- Bringing life to all

Rain is comforting

- Singing all to sleep

Rain is peaceful

- Nothing is as sweet

But like people, rain can turn against you

- Tearing down all in its
  path

Rain can become loud

- Making children cry

Rain can become dangerous

- Drowning the ones on the
  bottom

But the rain will stop and

The destruction will cease

- After the storm

It's what's lost during – that counts

I Go to You

For comfort, I come to you

For advice, I come to you

For understanding, I come to you

For love, I come to you

Now you must go

And I must let you

But please, don't go far

Because there is no one else

I can go to

Don't Forget Me

People grow and change
    They get new friends
And tend to forget the old
That's what's happening now
    And it scares me
    Because I am old
      And I don't want
To be forgotten

Change

Leaves change color in the fall
    Sports change all year long
Weather changes from hot to cold
    People change from job to job
Change is an everyday thing
    Then, why I ask, is change so scary

You Are Like Me

I wish I had what you had

Your carefree attitude

Your smiling face

There's always laughter

You seemed perfect

Then I saw you cry

And I wondered what happened

Finally, I realized, that you, like me,

Needed a friend to

Understand

That's why I am here now

I'm Sorry

You were always there for me

Listening, caring, giving

Then one day, when I needed you

You weren't there

I found you crying in your pillow

And I was mad

Because I needed you and

You weren't there

Now I realize my mistake

I was not the friend you

Needed me to be

The friend you always were to me

And I'm sorry

I Was Wrong

I did not mean to hurt you

That was not my intention

I was only trying to help

But I see now I was wrong

Now you cry because of me

Please forgive me

Real

You were there

It was not my imagination

I was not asleep

It was real

You were real

The laughter we shared was real

Your sweet smell was real

The smile on your face was
real

It's true

-    I've always dreamed of it

And today it came true

Yesterday/Today

Today with those lips you cursed me

Yesterday those lips told a different story

Yesterday they loved me

Yesterday they embraced mine

That was yesterday

Today is today

You can't go back to those yesterdays

And, hopefully, you won't remain in
today

You Still Do

Life will not cease just

Because you left

The world will not stop

Because you are gone
You are not the center of
The universe
I used to think you were
And for some reason
You still do

You're Confident

We're drifting apart
Going our own ways
And I'm scared
You never judge me
You always love me
You are my best friend
And what happens if you forget
The fun we had
The tears we shed
Or if I forget
The advice you gave
The hug you always had
I'm scared
But you're confident

So, I will trust you

And let go

I Watch You

I watch you

The way you move

The way you talk

The way you laugh

The way your face lights

Up when you smile

I watch everything

Mostly, though

I watch the way you

Look right through me

Light

You've always been my dream

But I lost hope

Now you smile at me

You talk with me

And that hope is coming back

A candle in my heart
Glows with new hope
Please, don't blow that light out

Help me

I want to play
That's all I have ever wanted
But there are limitations
That weren't there before
I can't overcome those limits
At least not by myself
Please, help me and let me play

Killing You

I will not cry
I will not mope
My heart has become hard
Towards you
I will not show my sadness
I will not let you see me dying inside
And in turn

I will be killing you

Me

I was not myself

    For so long

I did not laugh

    I did not smile

I lost my identify

I became a no one

    Just a body

        Empty and incomplete

But now, I have found

    That inner me

And it shows on the

    Outside

I am me

    And you can't take that

    At least, not anymore

Be Yourself

Be yourself, whatever you want to be

Then I want to be a bird
   and fly real high
Or a butterfly
   with beautiful wings
Or a tree
   with the wind in my arms
Or a blade of grass
   swaying in the breeze
I want to be so much
   But I can't because I
      don't know who I am
         now.

Not Worth It

What did you think

That I would sink

Beneath the ground

Just because you weren't around

Well, I didn't and I shan't

Really, I can't

You are not worth my tears

Or the mourning for years

You are nothing – that I now know
You were never love, only friendly foe
And to my heart you no longer link.

Already Dead

You can't hurt me anymore
You are unable to inflict pain
I will not cry because of you
I will not worry about you
You can't hurt me
    Nothing can
Because I am already dead.

Nothing in Return

I died the day you said goodbye
    I laid down and withered
For so long I was cold
    HE came though and breathed
      Into me
Now I breathe on my own
    I live on my own

And even though HE saved me

HE, unlike you, asks for nothing

In return

Stand Alone

You think you are so funny

I used to laugh at all you said

But that got old real fast

Now I no longer chuckle

And you stand alone

- Laughing

Lies

I thought it was love

- But it wasn't

I thought I was wrong

- But I was right

I thought I couldn't

- But I can

Things are different than they seem

I'm not who I appear to be

And you're not who you claim to be
Both of us are lying
To each other
But mostly, we are lying to ourselves

Chances

You cheated
and I gave you another change
You lied
and I gave you another chance
You were cruel
and I gave you another change
Chance after chance I gave you
Yet not once did you give me the chance
The chance to laugh
The chance to have fun
The chance to be myself
Now you are out of chances
And I have the chance I deserve
-    To live!

How Did You Do It

So much pain

    and still you laugh

So much confusion

    and still you are confident

So much anger

    and still you love

I never knew how

    you did it

But you reached out to me

    and now I know

You could laugh

    Be confident

      And love

Because you believed

    In yourself and the

      People around you

Thanks for showing me how

And thanks for believing in me

Friend

You listen to me

You comfort me

You laugh with me

You cry with me

You are my best guy friend

For me, though, that's where it stops

For you, though, there's so much more

Those hugs aren't just comfort

Those laughs aren't just cheerful

Those tears aren't just emotion

You see so much and want so much more

But you are only my friend

    And as a friend

I need you to do what you do best

        -    Understand

    That I can't

Forget

Don't you remember the laughter?

Don't you remember the fun?

How can you forget?

        -    this piece of your life?

How does anyone forget the one they loved?

Twice Suffering

For the longest time

    I dwelled on the laughter

    I remembered the fun

    I replayed the sweetness

And I forgot the pain

    I neglected the tears

    I erased the meanness

Never will I forget the good

And never, too, shall I exclude the bad

       -    I don't need to suffer
           twice

No More Tears

I can no longer cry

    One does not have so many tears

    All are shed and gone

- brought on by the
  cruelness of others
- dried by the warmth of
  friends

Someday I will look back

and cry once more

As soon as I store up enough tears

But until then I will block the memories

of what was lost

And look ahead to what can

be gained

Dreams – Yours & Mine

You are going away

With you, you take your dreams

Dreams of happiness and success

Also, with you, go my dreams

- my dream to see you
  smile
- my dream to see you
  succeed

- my dream of a path to
follow

Thank you for making dreams come true

Lessons

Thank you for showing me how to love

- how to laugh

- how to smile

and thank you for the best lesson ever

Thank you for teaching me to

be myself

- even if it means loosing

- the closest thing

to your heart

I will miss you

You've Changed

I watch you in disbelief

The way you've changed

You're a completely different person

What happened?

Why have you become so cruel?

You are no longer the one I loved

The one I cared for

You've changed

Why? You were perfect before

<u>Falling</u>

Like a brick, thrown from a building

    You fell

           -    hard

I, on the other hand,

    Am still drifting

              -    quite slowly

You are already where I am going

    But you got there so much faster

    And are trying to make me arrive sooner

    I want to drift

        and enjoy the flight

    I can't fall as fast as you

    Please; don't make me

Twice Suffer

No one wants to get hurt
>Including me

Yet hurt will come with life
>And I'll survive

>But why should I have to
>>suffer twice
>>>\-   for the same thing?

Ending It

I'm sorry that I hurt you
>I couldn't prevent it

>It was going to come

>The only question was
>>when and how bad

>And so I chose the day
>>to end it

The day that wouldn't hurt as much
>And I am sorry
>>but not regretting

They

They laughed
    and I walked away
They talked
    and I let them
Then they cried
    and I held their hand

Fools

It didn't come out like I meant it
It wasn't intended to be cruel
It was a statement
                -    plain and simple
Yet you took it wrong
    And it's your fault and mine
Yours for making me a fool
And mine for thinking you'd understand

Laughing

Was it supposed to hurt

-      what you said

Well, it didn't

     In fact

-      it made my day

Because all who heard

     Know everything

And they will be laughing,

     Just like you planned

        But not at me

        'Cause I'll be laughing too

        With them

         At you

You Don't Have It

How can you give someone

     what you do not have?

You can't give someone a dollar

     if you only have three pennies

So how can you give maturity

     if you, yourself, have none?

No Control

Was I supposed to cry?

Is that what you wanted?

Well then, cry I shall

Not because it hurts

Not because I care

Only because that's what you want

That's how it is, right?

That's how it used to be

But we're not in your world

are we?

And you have control over

nothing.

Nature's Job

You think that your words will help

All they do is hurt more

You cannot heal this wound with a kiss

It's bleeding and you cannot stop it

So, please, just let it alone

And allow nature to take its course

Good-Byes

It happened so fast

And came without warning

And I never got a

    chance to say

        good-bye

You have that chance

            -    Take it, cherish it, hold on
                  to it

I'll wait forever for my chance

    My only chance to

        say good-bye

Frailty

Fragileness kept her away

Not a game she could see

But after today

She'll be there, always, with HE

Whole

A part of you is gone

An emptiness inside you

Fill that void with memories

And be whole once again

Make Me

Wrap your arms around me

　　Make today disappear

Fold me into your torso

　　Make me feel safe

Kiss me gently

　　Make me feel wanted

Love me always

　　Make me whole

Would'a Could'a Should'a

They would have been friends

They could have laughed together

They should have had that chance

And now that they're both gone

    they can

Friends

Today I saw her smiling face

In another's eyes

It made me miss her more

Yet I was happy

Because I knew my grandma

Had another friend

Dear Grandma

    I'm at peace tonight

    Because I know she's with you

Take care of her

Guard her

Love her like we did

It is because of you and your

        strength

That I know she'll be okay

Chances

When I get the chance
       People become excited
Not because I'll dominate
Or even become essential
       People are excited
Because I've worked so hard to get here
And when my dream
       Becomes reality
They cheer with me; for me
It's those who don't work hard
And have always had that chance
That don't get cheered for
       That don't cheer for themselves
It's not a privilege to them
       It's a duty
And so they take the chance
       That's already expected
       And throw it away
Because it's expected to return again
       What if it didn't
       What if there wasn't another chance

Then they'd have no cheers
and no glory

Nothings

There are no words to make it right

Nothing expresses utter frustration

Nothing lessens the pain

Nothing can be done

And it's because of nothing that

You're frustrated

Nothing was done

Nothing was accomplished

And Nothing prevailed

Can't You See

Can't you see what you're doing

Destruction of self-esteem

Yours and others

Fighting amongst friends

Giving into foes

Can't you see that it's wrong

Best Friends

You are my best friend for many reasons
You listen, you help, you understand
You laugh and cry with me, not at me
You're there when I need you
You put things on hold, just for me
But most importantly, you're my best friend
Because you've never judged me – thanks

Was It

Was it love at first sight
No, it wasn't
Fairy tale romance
No, it isn't
Princess in a castle
No, she isn't
Knight on a white horse
No, he isn't
Moonlight walks
No, they aren't
Candle-lit dinners

No, they won't be

Perfect

Always and Forever

Be Free

I don't know what to do

Everyone has their advice

But it will not work for you

And I am trying so hard to be nice

I can't because it's not right

To neither you nor to me

So let's just stop this fight

And set each other free

Love vs. Like

You try so hard to make me happy

But happy, right now, is not something I can
be

I love you deeply and always will

Yet I'm not sure if I like you still

There is a difference between love and like

Love is an extremely long hike

It is pure and remarkable

Yet not often very obtainable

While like is a feeling inside your heart

That makes your blood-flow start

You can like and not love

But, I ask, can you not like but still love

Apology

I'm sorry that I push away

But my soul is very confused today

I can't tell right from wrong

My thoughts are so complicated and long

I apologize if I'm hurting you

But, in a way, I am hurting me too

Give Wings

I wish I knew

    What I could do

To give these things

    Beautiful wings

And send them away

    To ponder another day

Wasn't Sure

What's happening now is my fault

I never said what I wanted

And now I expect too much

I guess I wasn't sure

And now I'm even more confused

I can't explain, though I wish I could

Then both our minds would be at ease

Decision

Why can't someone just say…

    "Do this, go there"

Why can't someone make that decision

Because I can't do it on my own

    And no one seems willing to help

I Cannot

I cannot love like you do

I am not that strong

At least, not now

I am sorry that I fall short

Of the love you give me

I cannot return the

Devotion and Desire

As full and complete

As you give to me

I am not perfect

And I am sorry

Need You

You've always supported me

Even if it wasn't the best choice

You trusted me and gave good advice

Where are you now

When I need you most

For You

There is no way

That I can return

All that you have given me

The only thing I can do

Is try to make you proud

But I still need your guidance

Why are you so scared to give it

I am doing this for you

Old Man

When I looked into your eyes

I saw a fearful thing

-       an old man stared back

When did you age

Why have you grown so frail

Why do you frighten me so

Why must you remind me

That a father is still a mortal

You

You never second guess me

You always supported me

You've always loved me

You'd put your faith in me everyday

When did you stop believing in me

Fooled

I have fooled the world

Everyone sees something different

A role model, the perfect scholar

The best listener, an angel

So many things

They're all illusions

I am nothing of the sort

I have fooled the world

But not you

and yet you still

love me

Wrong

No matter what I say

    It seems wrong

        -   if not to you

        -   then to me

I am lost and scared

There is no way out

There is nothing I can do

Because everything will be wrong

Be It Kind

    I am sorry that you feel alone

There is nothing more that can be done

    I listen and try to understand

I give you hugs and pat your hand

    Sorry that it's not enough

But always being happy is really tough

    I hope that someday you will find

Whatever it is you're looking for

        -   be it kind

Love?

I thought it was love
But there were no butterflies in my
stomach when you walked in
Your touch never consumed me
and I never felt it deep in my soul
Your kiss did not overwhelm me
I can still think clearly
When I first saw you, there were no
fireworks, there was no music
I thought it was love
But now I don't know
I am so confused
Is this love?
And if it is
When will I know?

Constellation

At night, the sky fills with sparkles
Stars appear magically
Each star watches over an individual

shining ever so brightly

giving light when needed

illuminating her path when she is lost

providing hope when she becomes scared

Though she may not realize

where her strength originates

she feels an outside force

that of the star

Upon realizing the power

of her watchful star

she rises up and stands beside it

a constellation is born

All it takes is two stars

bonded by a force unknown to each

Friends, as well, are bonded by a force

Unknown to either, felt by both

The force of a star watches over us

We travel apart

Yet remain close

Because we wish upon the same star

Naming Stars

If I were to discover a star

I would name it after you

Because

You are beautiful

You are pure

You shine brightly

But mostly,

Because you are the light in my heart

Guiding me

Giving me hope

Allowing me to dream

Fortune Cookie

Hidden within the shell

Was a promise

As light passed the cracked seal

The stone glistened

A fortune lay within the cookie

A tale of love would unfold

If only he had given it

And if only she believed in Chinese
legends

Questions

How will I know

When will it become clear

Does anyone else know

Why won't they tell me

What is really happening

Will I ever find the secret

Face

Your angel face lures me

Because it is so delicate

Because it is so sincere

Because every feature calls me

But…..

I worry if you realize your power

If it is even your power at all

Or just my lack of power to change

Ifs

Your smile warms me

Just your presence fascinates me

You're in my mind

Day and night

When I think of you, I smile

I cannot control it

Yet you leave me alone to wonder

...if...

You notice my smile

You realize I am near

You ever think of me

So many "ifs" yet

I place my dreams on them all

Star's Gift

I wished upon a star one night

I wished, I wished, with all my might

The wish I wished one day came true

The day when I un-expectantly met you

I now had something to trust

And someone to go to if I must

A friendship bloomed that day

And continued to grow in every way

Your friendship has shown me so much

Love, compassion, trust, and such

I cherish all the laughter we've shared

And treasure all the times that you've cared

With you my tears would vanish

You'd make me smile when you spoke
Spanish

You've shown me what a friend should be

Most importantly, you showed me – me

Thank you my dear and trusting friend

And thank you star, for the gift that you did
send

Mystery

So much passion

So little compassion

Will the two ever equal

Or is the mystery in a sequel

I cannot live like this

Afraid that only a kiss
Will turn you into a crazed
Leaving me perpetually amazed
That one moment all I feel is love

Eyes

I have let you down
You won't admit it
But I hear it in your voice
And I see it in your eyes

Her

She's always had my ear and shoulder
I'll be okay, I always consoled her
But today when I needed her badly
Her ear and shoulder neglected me sadly
Her voice simply mocked me
Giving me the power to see
That though the friendship may seem strong
One single sweep and all will be wrong

Unheard

No matter how silly or absurd

I listened to your every word

Never once did I say you were wrong

Your tears I would never prolong

All of this I have given to you

I kinda expected it back too

But I was wrong and remain unheard

Tiny Sparkle

When you look at me

Your eye shines with a single sparkle

Such a small sign

Yet it fills me, making my blood boil

Everywhere I look

I see that tiny sparkle

My dreams are blinded

    By its light

The night fills with tiny sparkles

    Resembling your beautiful eyes

I never knew that such a tiny sparkle

Could ignite

Such a blazing flame

Right

I thought it was what you wanted

I also thought it's what I needed

Yet you question

And argue my motives

You are not satisfied

That's okay – I can handle that

But why on earth aren't you happy

I did the right thing

It's best for me

Butterfly

Like the wings of a butterfly

You lift me up

And give me strength

I trust in you

Depend upon your skill

Because I know you're there

I spread my wings

And take flight

Sharing

At night we'd just lay there –

Giggling in the dark

Telling secrets;

Sharing

I miss those days of closeness

But every now and then

She comes to me with a secret

Or I to her

And the sharing begins again

Oh, the sharing

That's the thing about sisters,

They are family – true

But more importantly;

They are friends; best friends

Transformation

She used to be dull;

Shy and unaware of her appearance

But now she has blossomed

And I envy her so

She is all together –

She knows what she wants and how to get
it

Where this transformation came from

Or how it happened

I don't know

Yet I do know that I am ready for it!

Teddy Bear

Like an old teddy bear

Worn with use,

Yet huggable and kind,

A good listener,

A caretaker,

Trusting and hopeful,

Understanding and forgiving,

Sharing in my joys, my dreams, my
sadness

Like an old teddy bear

That is always there –

Is you; my mother; my friend

Love Is A Toy

Love is like one of those wind-up cars

Starting off in such a hurry

Going strong for a while

Not knowing how long it will last

Final Tears

Trumpets ring in a glorious greeting

> The rest of the band soon follows

Utter chaos and confusion takes over as each

> Section goes their separate ways

Then suddenly –

> It is quiet

The clarinets begin to lull you to sleep;

> The beautifully performed sax solo
> relaxes your entire body;

> You begin to drift

The blast of a trumpet brings you back to
reality

As the rest of the band joins in, the sound
indicates happiness

> But somewhere a tuba is mourning

> A tuba not playing the happy tune the
> others play

> A tuba expressing its sadness in the midst
> of all the joy

The tuba is playing by itself now

> Mourning to itself

Now, the band begins to mourn with it

> The last note is the tuba's final tear

Stranger

His eyes seem to wander;

> Looking for something;

Suddenly, his eyes light up;

> As if he found that certain something.

His long stride carries him swiftly across the
floor

> He seems to float

Now, as he looks down upon me I see a

Hint of sadness in his eyes

The once brilliant twinkle fades

He recognizes me but I don't know

Who he is

As he becomes more overwhelmed with
sadness

I feel connected to him

Why or how, I don't know

But the connection is there

The sad eyes grow red with determination

He pulls me close as if the closer I get

The more I'll understand

At his touch, I collapse with relief into

My brother's arms

I remember him!

Life

In the sunlit woods

A flower begins to bloom

Who gave this great life

Confusion

Confusion is like a funhouse full of mirrors

Lost and alone

Gray and wispy

Crying for a way out

Help me

Soft Sounds

Soft sounds that echo in my heart

A child's joyful laughter

Quiet tears of joy

Whispers of encouragement in the wind

Birds chirping in the spring

Such soft sounds carry much meaning

Tis Better To Give Than to Receive

Tis better to give than to receive, that's what they always say

And so I try to give, day by day

A Good Luck card here, a Birthday card there

It seems as if I'm the only one to care

All birthdays and special occasions I cover

I update my calendar, always I hover

Over it to see

What tomorrow shall be

Giving is supposed to make you feel better

Even if it's only a silly letter

But for me it hurts so much to know

I have no true friends, only friendly foe

Yeah, so they may say thanks, they may

Even if they do, it still ruins my day

To know I'll get nothing in return

Not a card, a teddy bear, or even dying fern

Tis better to give than receive

If that's how it is – I'd better leave

Tracks

Ever been on a long trip, not knowing what to do?

Here's a little game I play

On that long, traveling day

Listen closely as I explain it to you

Every time you go over a railroad track

Whether one, three, or two

Hold up your feet and touch a screw

It takes some practice, but soon you'll get the nack

Now close your eyes

Hold 'em tight

Think with all your might

And wish a wish you know is wise

It's a real great game

To play in the car

Even if your trip isn't very far

Wish for a strangers, or name 'em by name

I was playing one day

This game of fun

And wishing for a special someone

To get better, I probably should have begun to pray

Every track we crossed

I'd touch a screw

It was the only thing I could do

And wish for a miracle, that the ill wouldn't
be lost

And then the dread became the facts

On this day

I hate to say

There weren't enough tracks.

Tears

Sometimes, I feel so alone,

    I cry

Sometimes, I feel so helpless,

    I cry

Sometimes, I feel so sick,

    I cry

Sometimes, I feel so happy,

    I cry

I cry for many reasons, but the tears I shed

    tonight are shed for only one reason

Rejection

Friendship

Friendship is unconditional

Friendship is pure

Friendship is caring

Friendship is listening

Friendship is comforting

Friendship is trying

Friendship is trusting

Friendship is love

Friendship is hard

> and I'm glad we get to go through it
> together

Does this make sense to you?

Does this make sense to you?

I used to be cruel, selfish, and I had the

> temper of the Grand Canyon

Yet I had friends out the wazoo!

Now, over the years, I've changed

I have controlled my temper, I have become less

selfish, I have begun to say "hi" to people

I don't know

I have changed for the better, I feel

Yet, now, I have no friends

Does this make sense to you?

I feel better about myself, I think I have become

a better person,

yet all my friends have left me

Does this make sense to you?

Hero

I made him out to be a hero

He taught me all I knew

He helped me; understood me

He was my knight in shining armor

But now, as I look back

He was never there

He taught me nothing

He wasn't there to help me up when I fell

He wasn't even there when I didn't need help

He was and still is my hero

But he

Never cared

Short Glory

It feels like you've been in the same position forever

Crouched low, hands out stretched

You are anticipating a hit

Right at you

You know you can do it

The ball comes

Right at you

You step into it

It projects off the platform your arms have made

The ball goes up

A perfect pass

Right to the setter

Now for the finishing touch

You wait back, ready to accelerate

The set is low, you'll to have to hurry

You take your approach

    Right

    Left

       Right, left

You're in the air

    Bam

The ball strikes the floor

    An Ace!

Now as gravity pulls you down

    your feet become tangled

       You fall

         Crack!

           The pain!

              Your glory is over

"He Said"

He said he'd never hurt a friend

    Never forget a friend

    Never betray a friend

I asked him if I was his friend

    He said I was

So I asked him why he hurt me

He never answered

A Lost Cause

I dreamt about him at night

envisioned his face throughout the day

I believed he liked me

But I was afraid

So, I let her call him

We all went out

But it was obvious

He had trouble talking to me

But with her, words flowed like a waterfall

Crushing me

She was my friend

He was my dream

Now, I've lost them both

Perfection

He's got everything

All I have ever wanted

and more than I could imagine

He's perfect

His smile makes me melt

His voice, its own music

His eyes dance with life when he's happy

His laughter, a piece of chocolate

deep, sweet, and delicious

He's perfect; too perfect for me

Sand Castle

A friendship is a lot like a child on the beach

with a plastic pail and shovel

The child packs sand into the pail like a friend

packs trust into a friendship

If the sand is loosely packed, it will not hold, just as

a loose piece of trust will fall

A child who wants the best caste will build it large,

luxurious, and fast, asking the tiny sand grains a lot

Also, the friend who puts too many demands on a

friendship will crush it under its weight

Someone

All I want is someone

Someone to love me no matter what

Someone to put their arms around me and rock me to sleep

Someone to talk to who'll listen and understand

Someone to make me laugh

Someone to give me a hug just because

Just Someone to love

That's all I want

Little Boy

There once was a little boy

A bail full of laughs

A glowing smile

The cutest boy in the world

I loved that little boy

But one day God decided that little boy had
done his job

        and took him home

I miss that little boy

    That laughter

    That smile

    That cute little boy

I don't blame God for taking him –

    I blame only myself

        for not loving him more

love?

He asked me if I loved him

I told him I didn't know what love was

    But....

if love is laughing, I love him

if love is thinking about him all the time, I
love him

if love is getting goose bumps when he
brushes your shoulder, I love him

if love is a ray of sunshine in your day, I love
him

if love is trusting someone, I love him

if love is waiting all day for one hug, I love
him

if love is kisses and smiles, I love him

if love is happiness, I love him

if love is tickle wars and frosting fights, I love
him

if love is chocolate; deep, rich, and
irresistible, I love him

if love is dreaming about him, I love him

if love is sweet and unpredictable, I love him

if love is turning to mush when he winks at
you, I love him

    love can be so many things

and if this is love

       I'm going to hold on to it

          for a long while

Thoughts

What are you thinking?

I'm thinking how much I like you

I'm thinking about the way I feel when you
touch me,

    when you look at me

when you smile

when you wink at me

when you hold me

I'm thinking about how much crap you take from me

my moods swings

my sarcastic remarks

my constant whining

my inability to express my feelings

I'm thinking about tomorrow and what it will bring

possibly an A on my essay

possibly a fight with a friend

possibly a letter from a friend

hopefully, time with you

I'm thinking about how cute

how sweet

how funny

how adorable

how likeable you are

I'm thinking that someday I'll do something dumb and lose you forever

I'm thinking how afraid I am

Of what? Of losing you. Of saying the
wrong thing

I'm thinking about the songs on the radio

Could that be me and you; happy and
content

Or

What if that were to happen to us

I'm thinking about a lot of stuff

So much, in fact, it's hard to figure it all out
sometimes

But mostly, I'm thinking about how much I
like you

I Love Him

There's this guy

this incredible guy

He's the sweetest, cutest, best-est guy

I love him with all my heart

It took me forever to say it, but it's true

I love him

He doesn't realize this

In fact, he denies that I love him

It bothers me; that he questions my feelings

I finally said what was on my mind

and instead of accepting what I said,

he refuses to listen and believe

Well, believe it, buddy

I love you!

Forever Hug

I could lay there all day and night

through the spring, summer, fall, and
winter

through the rain, hail, fog, sleet, and snow

through tornados and earthquakes

watching movie after movie

watching artificial grass grow

watching paint dry

I could lay there

In a forever hug

I Don't Know

"I don't know" is often the best answer
because

if you say something false just to have an
answer,

it'll be wrong

if you ignore the question

they'll think you're deaf

if you say nothing

they'll think you're hiding something

if you say what they want to hear

it's not true

So, if you're asked a question and you don't
know the answer

Say, "I don't know"

It may not solve the problem

but at least

it'll be true

Questions

Friend – or – Foe?

Yes – or – No?

True – or – False

Black – or – White

Too many questions are spinning

Out of control

In my head

I can't answer them all and

There's no one to help me

Like a Balloon

Like a balloon, full of air,

I sit here

When it's warm, I am full of life

But when you take that balloon out,

into the cold,

it deflates

and

withers

Will you please hand me a blanket?

I'm cold

So cold.

Red

Red is such a bright color

such a happy color

It can mean so many things
> Health, love, happiness; life

But people change the meaning too much
> Embarrassment, hate, humiliation; hell
>> Why?
>>> Why are people so cruel?

Tumbling

A tumble. A fall.
> A tear.
>> A cry.

It's not funny.
> So, why are you laughing?

I Need You

I'm lying here. In all my blankets –
> a snug, warm hug.

The heater blows warm all around –
> Caressing me

The radio sings its lullaby,
> Rocking me gently

The walls of my room, like a castle guard,
protect me,

    From thieves and snow storms

And yet I'm awake –

       Why?

    I miss you, I need your goodnight

    Your sweet, adorable, goodnight

      I need that; I need you –

        to go to sleep

So, if there were no blankets

    no heater

    no radio

    no walls

I'd be okay

    but only if you are here.

Can I Keep It?

The boy brings home a turtle from the pond

    Can I keep it? he asks

A girl catches a butterfly

    Can I keep it? she begs

    A stray dog along the road;

A baby bird in the nest;

A toad in the grass;

A caterpillar on a leaf;

We all ask ourselves, Can I keep it?

In that turtle with its adorable smile

that butterfly is beautiful and free

that dog, all friendly and cute

that bird, its voice; music

that toad, lovable and full of life

that caterpillar is cozy and warm

In these, I see you.

And like that boy and that girl I wonder

Can I keep it?

A Wish

If I could have anything at all, what would it
be?

This is a wish, an anything wish

What would it be?

I could wish for money, become rich and have
everything.

But you can't buy what I really want

I could wish for health and live forever

>   But that would get lonely

I could wish for wisdom

>   But then I couldn't ask you for help

I could wish for friends

>   But I like choosing my own

I could wish for the power to read minds

>   But what if you hated me

I could wish for so much

>   But it won't be what I want

Because all I want is you;

>   holding me, your breath, so warm on my cheek

>   >   that's all I want;

>   >   >   the chance to hold you forever.

Expression of Emotion

Crying is an expression of emotion

There are tears of happiness

>   -   when you're overcome with joy

There are tears of confusion

- when there's nothing else
to do

There are tears of frustration

- when nothing seems to
work

There are tears of determination

- when there's a cause
worth fighting for

There are tears of anger

- when someone does
something wrong

This part is simple; tears are an expression of emotion

Deciphering that emotion is what's tough

Why

Why did you hurt me?

I know you don't know that you did

But I hurt and it's because of you

It's partly my fault too

I should let it pass and not worry

But I can't

I can't get it out of my head

I wish I could

But it won't let go

So, I ask myself why did you hurt me

and why did I let you?

Forever Because of You

It was a knife in my side

A bullet in my leg

A fly in my salad

A bone in my chicken

It was a shock; unexpected and frightful

The knife wound will heal

The bullet removed and the leg mended

The fly can be picked out and the salad replaced

The bone is an obstacle which is easily removed

But the hurt of the wounds and the thought of the fly and bone

Remain forever

Always, in the back of my mind

And there; lies today

All the hurt that it brought

All the confusion too

Always and forever; are my feelings –
bleeding and hurt

Because of you

Gifts

It was a gift

A special gift

It made me feel special too

Not because it was a present

Because it was from you

You give me gifts everyday

It's like Christmas when I'm with you

A smile; wrapped in a bow

A wink; in big boxes and small

A hug; like a real live teddy bear

All these are gifts

Gifts from the heart

And that' where they go –

Straight to my heart;

Treasured forever

Feelings

Feelings are a delicate thing
They can hurt for many reasons
Maybe because no one said hi
> or because you feel yucky inside
> or because you don't understand why
> or because no one will leave you alone
> or because you're afraid

Trying to understand them is tough
> But explaining them is even harder
> > Especially to the someone that hurt
> > you

How Can I?

How can I tell you what's wrong?
How can I tell you what hurts?
How can I tell you why I'm sad?
How do I explain to you the problem?
How do you tell anyone it's them?
> That they're the reason you hurt, the
> reason you cry

How can I tell you; it's you?

Broken

What was that?

That agonizing sound

That horrendous scene

It was loud as thunder

But I could hear a pin drop

It was very dark

But I'm blinded by the light

What happened?

A heart, a living, pumping heart;

soft and warm; alive and full;

just broke.

It snapped in two

It's hurting and bleeding now

The blood a trail of fire in my body

The heart is growing cold

Save it!

All it needs is a hug

One hug and it'll seal and thrive again

That's all it needs; all *I* need

Just one hug

Please, Understand

I'm crying on the inside
    on the outside too
I didn't know a person could cry so much
    could ache so much
I didn't know I had that many tears
    I do now and so do you
You turned on those faucets
    I need you to turn them off
to say you understand

You Knew

I'm hurting
    and you know why
        you caused it
    and you knew it would hurt me
So, why did you still do it?

What can I do

I worry when you're sick

And wonder what I can do to help

I could make you soup

Chicken noodle cures everything

I could rub your neck

Relax and maybe you'll feel better

I could leave you alone

If that would help

I could just sit and watch you sleep

That would help me

I could and would do anything to make
you feel better

Please tell me

What can I do

Because I Love You

I was worried and scared last night

You looked so sick and fragile

And there was nothing I could do to
help

All I could do was watch you sleep

    Each breath you took a prayer

That God would help you get better

    Because you are my dearest friend

    Because you are the one I go to when I
    am down

    Because you always have a smile to share

And because; I love you

Smile to Share

You always have a smile to share

    and I crave that smile

Every time I see your smile

    the day's events disappear

Like the sun after the rain

    Your smile dries my tears

No matter how bad your day was

    You always have a smile to share

Thanks for sharing

I Didn't Get To

I didn't get to see you today

I didn't get to hold you

I didn't get to kiss you

I didn't get to watch your every move

That may sound dumb, but each day I wish

> to see you
>
> to hold you
>
> to kiss you
>
> to watch you

I wait and wait and today I had to wait for eternity

I'm still waiting – 'till tomorrow

When I can wrap my arms around you

> and love you forever

Some Girls

Some girls wish for roses and chocolate

Some want jewelry and gifts

Some just want happiness and love

You are my rose; sweet smelling and delicate

You are my chocolate; sweet and irresistible

The twinkle in your eye shines brighter than any gem

Your smile is the best gift possible

With you I find endless happiness

You are love

And that's all I want

You

Did I Say Five

My five senses can sense you

My eyes see you; perfect and gorgeous

My ears hear you; incredibly sweet and sincere

My noses recognizes your intoxicating smell

My hands reach out to hold you

My lips yearn for one sweet-tasting kiss

My five senses are in love with you

Did I say five – there's one more

My heart

Aching for you

That makes six

All are in love with you

And, so am I

I Missed You

I missed you today

I missed your presence

I missed your smile

I missed your laugh

I missed your kisses

I missed your voice

And because I love your presence

Because I love your smile

Because I love your laugh

Because I love your kisses

Because I love your voice

Because I love you

I missed you today

Snowflakes

Every time I am not with you, I miss you

> I look forward to your smile, your laugh,
> your kisses

They are a part of my day

> And today was all cut up

> > Like a child's paper snowflake

> Pieces were missing; you were missing

But tomorrow is a new day and a new piece of
paper

> I hope the scissors are not there

Deer

I was a deer in the headlights today

> Scared and alone

But it was not a car that scared me

> In fact, it was a lack of something

> > The lack of you

You were not where I expected you to be

> And that froze me

But I called you; the ringing on the phone, a
car's horn

I became aware of my surroundings

And got off the road

Thanks for honking the horn

Expectations

You were not where I expected you to be

You weren't by my side

And I hated you so

But I know now, I expected too much

And I am sorry

Please, don't do the same

Don't hate me

How Do You Say

How do you say I love you

Some use words

But I am tongue tied

Some use flowers

But I don't know which to send

Some use candy

But I am not sure what you like

I don't know how to say I love you

    All I do know is that I do

And all I can do is hope you understand

I Want To, But I Can't

I am here, thinking of you

    I want to see you, but I can't

    I want to talk to you but I can't

    I want to hold you but I can't

    I want to be with you but I can't

    I want to kiss you but I can't

And because I can't, I sit here

    Waiting until the day I can

Fear

Fear is the worst feeling there is

    And today, fear races through my blood;
    scorching my being

I am afraid that I have lost you

I am afraid that you don't love me anymore

I am afraid of what will happen

I am afraid of what has already happened

And I am alone in my fear

    Because you are not here

Tornado

I am trapped in a tornado

    I don't know which way is up

    I can't see anything

    I don't know where I am

    I don't even know who I am anymore

    I am scared and alone; that I know

And as the song goes;

    Where do I go from here

Alone

I was born into this world alone

I will die alone

What happens in between is my choice

And I choose to not be alone

But I am

Even with you, I am alone

Alone in my thinking

Alone in my feelings

Alone in the world

I do not want to be alone

I try so hard not to be

But I am

And there's nothing I can do

Except ask you to stay

You Were Here

Today was a day

Filled with smiles

Bubbling over with laughter

Packed with fun

All because you were here

Storybook

I am trapped in a storybook

And everywhere I look

I see smiles and hear laughter

I hope to live 'happily ever after'

It's time for me to meet my prince

Turn the page, go ahead – you've waited ever since

To read the very happy ending

Now there's no more pretending

Because, on the last page you will see

Quite happily

You and me

Volcano

A volcano erupted today

Stored up feelings ran hot, like lava

Destroying everything in its path

Including the wall, built to block it out

All I can do is watch the wall crumble

And pray it doesn't get to the important thing

My love for someone special

Old Toy

I feel like an old toy

Thrown in the toy box

Forgotten forever

Just Once

Just once I want someone to say

it's okay, it's not your fault

Just once I want someone to hold me

and tell me everything's going to be fine

Just once I want someone to take my side

and not blame me

Just once I want someone to say

that they'll love me even if I mess up

Just once I want someone to understand

Just once

Three Tiny Words

They can crush a person

Or lift them up

Three tiny words

They can scare a person

Or fill them with happiness

Three tiny words

They are treasured in our hearts

In our mind and soul, they remain

Three tiny words

They can make a person cry

Or laugh out loud

Three tiny words

These three tiny words may seem insignificant
to you

But they mean the world to me

Those three tiny words

Memories

A new beginning

another chance

a look into the future

a step ahead

a scary thought

But, luckily, we can take with us, the
memories

those precious memories

In those memories

    the happiness you've brought me

    the laughter we've shared

    the games we've played

    the fun we had

As I look back, into those memories

    I hope that this new beginning isn't all
    new

    because I want you right where you are

        beside me

           making more memories

With Or Without

You sit next to me

    and yet I am alone

I try to touch you

    but you don't want me to

    or, if you do, you advance not

So, I leave and let you alone

    now you will know how I feel

    because I am alone

With or without you
    lately, though, it's been
      without you

I can't

I can't do this anymore
    I can't pretend
You don't love me
    You may never have
    I don't know
But I can't keep this up
    I can't laugh it off
    I have cried too much for that now
So, I leave you
    And go my own way
That, I can do

Goodbye

Goodbyes have always hurt
But none like today's
The hurt today is deadly

But must be inflicted

To set you and me free

Goodbye

You Believed

You believed in me

From the moment you first saw me

You believed in me

Even before I could walk or talk

You believed in me

And because you believed, I did too

Now look what I have done and
accomplished

All because you believed in me

Thank You Daddy

When I learned to walk

You held my hand and showed me how

When I learned to talk

You were there, babbling along with me

When I first tried to ride a bike

You kissed my knees when I fell and put me back on

When I struck out for the first time

Your hand was on my head and your words kept me from giving up

When I hit my first homerun

It was your victory too

When I got hurt

Your strong arms carried me

When I did the right thing

It was your teachings that helped me decide

When I went on my first date

You paced the floors

When I first got my heart broken

You were ready to fight the world for me

You have always been there, Dad

And in the future, you will be there too

Because

When I go to college

I'll need help with all the decisions

When I get married

I'll need someone to give me away

When I'm lonely, afraid, or confused

    I'll need your guidance

I know I don't say this often, but I love you
Daddy

    And thank you, for loving me

Tomorrow

You used to like holding my hand

You used to like watching movies with me

You used to like kissing me

You used to say you love me

That was yesterday

Today you don't see me

Today you decide you hate movies

Today you don't kiss me

Today you don't even like me

Yesterday is gone – today is today

And tomorrow is new

Where Are You

You talk to me and yet say nothing

You look at me, but see through me

You used to speak volumes

You used to see portraits

What has changed

Where is your voice

Where are your eyes

Where are you

Friends

You said you wanted to be friends

Were you telling the truth

Because

Friends talk

Friends laugh

Friends share

Friends are there for you

You said you wanted to be friends

What is your definition of friends

Love

Love is not a faucet
>You can't turn it on
>>Use it
>Then turn it off
It doesn't work that way
>Neither do I

Coaster

Telling you my feelings is a roller coaster

It's scary, but once you get over that first big hill, it's okay

That's how it is with me

I have to gain courage to tell you

Gain trust of your strength to confide in you

That's the hill, once over it, feelings flow like the rest of the ride

>Fast and smooth

Like that coaster, there is a line to wait in

I guess the line was too long for you

A Taste of Heaven

Heaven is a glorious place

A place of belonging

A place of love

A place where there are no worries

There are no fears

Everything is happy and content

There is a peace within

Heaven is perfect

And every time you hold me

    I get a taste of heaven

The Point

I have changed for you

I am no longer energetic and spontaneous

I run on your schedule and you alone

I have become your vision of perfection

But now you don't want it anymore

You want adventure

    A more outgoing gal

But I can't go back

    I've forgotten it all

    I forgot who I am

    You've taken that from me

    My identity, my life

It's all gone and for what

    Just to be accepted

But you no longer accept me anymore

    So, what was the point

        What is the point now

Destroyed

They seemed perfect

Nothing was wrong

    At least, not on the outside

But inside was a bull

    In a China shop

    Breaking and destroying

All that was beautiful

Now, all that remains

    is rubble

Broken glass cuts away the inside

destroying all that is good

Her

You look at her like you used to look at me
With complete admiration and adoration
You admire her sense of humor
And adore her sensual beauty
That used to be me; but now it is her
I have been replaced, that I can see
But you are so blinded by her
That you do not see me;
Being torn apart – piece by piece
But it's okay, I am leaving now
You don't have to worry
I'll be okay and you, two, will be okay

Happy

Happiness is a state of mind
    that I can no longer find
All that was good is gone;
    like the grass clippings on the lawn

Blown away in the breeze

help me, I say, help me please

To find what I lost

it doesn't matter the cost

I wish to be happy once more

so leave, and close the door

This Truth

I thought I could handle it

But I can no longer ignore it

this truth you held

It stabs at my heart

And explodes in my brain

this truth you held

I am dying now; inside and out

Because of this

this truth you withheld

The Heart

The heart is very strong

It can endure so much pain

It can consume so much hate

And it keeps beating

But even the strongest heart

Can't wait forever

Can't pretend forever

Can't understand forever

Can't ignore forever

Can't forget

A heart is strong, but it can't do it all alone

It needs love to keep on beating

Your love

And your strength

Love Hurts

Love is the greatest feeling in the world

It fills you with utter joy

It takes up that void in your being

It enriches your soul

That is love

And so I ask you

If love is so great and this is love

Then why do I hurt so much

Cry so much
Because love, too, hurts

There is Hope

Flowers no longer bloom
   they wilt and die
Birds no longer fly
   they fall to the ground
The life is gone
   the love forgotten
But there is hope
   plant a seed and teach them to fly
Bring back that life
   remember the love
And cherish both

Different

God made me
God made you
   differently

Nothing Left

I have cried

I have pleaded

I have kept quiet

I have thrown tantrums

There is nothing left to do

I cannot make you understand

So I leave you with your thoughts

Maybe then you will see what I was saying

First Love

The first love it the hardest

    The hardest to find

    The hardest to understand

    The hardest to open up to

But most of all the first love

    is the hardest to leave

Stampede

Nowhere to run

Nowhere to hide

I am alone in a stampede

    Getting crushed

        dying

You opened the gates

    And let the bulls out

Now you watch

        in mere pleasure

Shut Out

I wanted to play

    They said I wasn't good enough

I wanted to cry

    They said I shouldn't

I wanted to sleep

    They wouldn't let me

I wanted to run

        They held me back

I wanted to leave

    They made me stay

They have shut me out for so long

    Now all I want is to shut them out

But they won't let me

Soaring

I take a risk in this thing
I spread my fragile wing
And soar so high
The trees below pass by
So fast
Then there's that awful blast
Now comes the pain
Again and again
White feathers, stained in red
Fall peacefully to the riverbed
A life is lost and it's so unfair
Because the hunter doesn't care

Not Just Me

It's not just me
    I thought it was
But they see it too
    The way you are

Uncaring and cruel
They comment and joke
That's how it is
How it's always been
Now I know
It wasn't just me

Ha Ha

It is a joke
the whole thing
You laugh about it
they laugh along with you
This is a joke
you and I are a joke
I am glad you find it so funny

Nothing

You think you are so great
You are all wonderful
I used to believe that too
I used to think that I wasn't good enough

But I was wrong and so are you

Because you are nothing

Nothing

Doormat

On the ground

collecting dust

I lay silently

Your footprints are heavy on my being

walking, stomping, scuffing

When I wear out, you will just throw me away

in the pile, along with the other doormats

forgotten forever

Ten Little Fingers

We have ten little fingers

Unscarred, Unbroken

Ten perfect little fingers

That reach for you

For reassurance

For comfort

For protection

As our fingers grow

They may get a scar or two

They may break a time or two

But they'll always reach for you.

You gave us our little fingers

And you'll help us make them strong

So that one day

When we have ten little fingers reaching for us

For reassurance

For comfort

For protection

We'll know what to do

Because you taught us.

Godmother

My Mommy and Daddy chose you

Because you are Special

Because they believe in you

Because they know you will show

Me the way of the Lord

You are my Godmother

Through you I will learn to love

Learn to be selfless

Learn to be who God made me

Thank you for agreeing

To guide me

To light my path

To love me

You are my Godmother

Quilt

May this quilt be a reflection of your life together

A representation of the family you built

And a dedication to the love you have given.

Our family was built on a foundation

May the corner squares remind you of these building blocks.

First, the home you gave us – was strong,
secure and safe

The birds in flight is our greatest feat –
because of you, we were able to spread our
wings

The love you gave us unconditionally – is
seen in the corner heart

And it all began with your steps to the altar –
and this square anchors the quilt.

In your forty years, you raised three children

> The remainder of the quilt are your
> children.

The eldest chose the Family Crest

> Because you gave us tradition

> Protected us like the shield

> And taught us the meaning of family.

The middle child chose the Crown of Thorns

> For giving us faith – in God, you, and
> ourselves

> And for demonstrating God's love in all
> you do.

The youngest chose the Card Trick

> Because you taught us the rules of the
> game – in sports, cards and, in life

> As well as the grace to accept victory

And the humility to accept defeat.

These three squares are as different as your children

But together may they embrace you

Keep you warm at night

And be a daily reminder of how much you are loved

My Sister

As little girls, we would dream about our wedding days

Maybe picturing our current beau in a tux at the end of the aisle

These details would change

We dreamed of the flower, the cake, and the music

All changing as our moods shifted

So many things to consider, so many decisions

Who would carry the rings

Who would play the organ

Who would cater the reception

As life took us on our journey

Almost every detail changed

But there was one constant

And that was you

Because,

no matter who made the cake

or who carried the rings

no matter where the reception was held

or where the honeymoon would take place

You were always in my mind – right beside
me

Because I knew

you would look lovely

you would share in my joy

you would comfort my fears

and you would stand next to me

as I took that next step

For that, my sister, I thank you

Patience

Her name was Patience

At least that is what he taught her

Have patience and it will come out right

He taught her algebra at four

She wasn't sure how; but she knew the
answers

"Have patience and one day you will know
why"

was all he said

He taught her the rules of the game

Before the rest of the girls understood

"But dad, a caught popup requires the girls to
go back"

"Have patience, the others will learn soon
enough"

"Daddy, I didn't get asked to the dance"

"Have patience, you will find Mr. Right"

In college, she struggled to find her niche

"Have patience, you are on the right path"

Being the youngest, she always felt left
behind

"Have patience, your time will come"

Today is her day, she slips on her wedding
gown

Her father comes in, ready to escort her

"Daddy, have patience, I am not quite ready to
let go"

CARA BABEL

CPSIA information can be obtained
at www.ICGtesting.com
Printed in the USA
BVOW03s1327010917
493780BV00001B/1/P